Civilizations of the World
MAYA CIVILIZATION

by Allison Lassieur

FOCUS READERS
NAVIGATOR

WWW.FOCUSREADERS.COM

Copyright © 2020 by Focus Readers, Lake Elmo, MN 55042. All rights reserved. No part of this book may be reproduced or utilized in any form or by any means without written permission from the publisher.

Focus Readers is distributed by North Star Editions:
sales@northstareditions.com | 888-417-0195

Produced for Focus Readers by Red Line Editorial.

Content Consultant: Thomas Garrison, Assistant Professor, Department of Anthropology, Ithaca College

Photographs ©: Diego Grandi/Shutterstock Images, cover, 1, 25; soft_light/Shutterstock Images, 4–5; meunierd/Shutterstock Images, 6; Peter Hermes Furian/Shutterstock Images, 8; marcosdominguez/Shutterstock Images, 10–11; Richard Maschmeyer/Alamy, 13; ahau1969/Shutterstock Images, 15; Chronicle/Alamy, 16–17; Rafal Cichawa/Shutterstock Images, 19; Lanmas/Alamy, 20; J. Enrique Molina/Alamy, 22–23; Yobab/Shutterstock Images, 27; Joern Haufe/Getty Images News/Getty Images, 29

Library of Congress Cataloging-in-Publication Data
Names: Lassieur, Allison, author.
Title: Maya civilization / by Allison Lassieur.
Description: Lake Elmo, MN : Focus Readers, [2020] | Series: Civilizations of the world | Audience: Grades 4-6. | Includes bibliographical references and index.
Identifiers: LCCN 2019006119 (print) | LCCN 2019006773 (ebook) | ISBN 9781641859660 (pdf) | ISBN 9781641858977 (ebook) | ISBN 9781641857598 (hardcover) | ISBN 9781641858281 (pbk.)
Subjects: LCSH: Mayas--History--Juvenile literature. | Mayas--Social life and customs--Juvenile literature. | Mexico--Civilization--Juvenile literature. | Central America--Civilization--Juvenile literature.
Classification: LCC F1435 (ebook) | LCC F1435 .L37 2020 (print) | DDC 972/.6--dc23
LC record available at https://lccn.loc.gov/2019006119

Printed in the United States of America
Mankato, MN
May, 2019

ABOUT THE AUTHOR

Allison Lassieur is the author of more than 150 nonfiction books on history, science, culture, technology, and current events. She also writes novels, puzzle books, activity books, and games. She lives in upstate New York with her husband, daughter, three dogs, a cat, and more books than she can count.

TABLE OF CONTENTS

CHAPTER 1
Meet the Maya 5

CHAPTER 2
Religion and Rulers 11

CHAPTER 3
Daily Life 17

CHAPTER 4
Rise and Fall 23

CONTRIBUTIONS
Maya Calendars 28

Focus on Maya Civilization • 30
Glossary • 31
To Learn More • 32
Index • 32

CHAPTER 1

MEET THE MAYA

In the Maya city of Chichen Itza, people streamed to the playing field. A game of *pitz* was about to begin. Tall walls stood at either side of the huge field. Crowds sat along the walls to watch. Two teams marched onto the flat field. Each team had two to three players. They wore helmets, pads, and chest protection.

Some *pitz* fields, such as this one in the city of Uxmal, had stone hoops on the sides.

 Many *pitz* fields, such as this one in the city of Copan, were long and flat.

Stone hoops hung near the top of each wall. Players tried to send a large rubber ball through one of the hoops. They used their hips to move the ball. The crowd cheered for their favorite team. But *pitz* was more than a game. It was also a religious event. At the end of the game, one team would be **sacrificed** to the gods.

Pitz was an important part of life for the Maya people. The Maya have lived in Mexico and Central America for more than 2,000 years. This **civilization** was at its height between the years 250 and 950 CE. At one time, it covered more than 120,000 square miles (311,000 sq km).

WORKING WITH RUBBER

A *pitz* ball was about the size of a volleyball. A few ancient *pitz* balls have been found. The balls are among the oldest examples of objects made of rubber. To make rubber, the Maya mixed sap from the rubber tree with juice from morning glory plants. They used this mixture to make the bouncy balls. The Maya also made rubber sandals.

The Maya built large cities throughout their lands. Thousands of people lived in

MAYA CIVILIZATION

The Maya civilization covered three main areas.

these cities. Tikal, the capital city, had a population of 60,000 people. Maya cities had temples, pyramids, and palaces. They also had *pitz* fields and monuments to gods and local rulers.

The Maya civilization did not have a single king or emperor. Instead, it was made up of many city-states. Each of these city-states was like a tiny independent country. It had its own ruler and government. A city-state's ruler controlled the city and the land around it. Rulers protected and provided for the people who lived there. Each ruler had a group of advisors. They helped the ruler make decisions.

CHAPTER 2

RELIGION AND RULERS

Religion had a major influence on life in Maya cities. The Maya worshipped many gods. They believed that the god Itzamná created humans and gave them writing. Other gods were related to nature. For example, Ah Mun was the god of corn. Chaac was the god of rain.

The giant pyramid in the city of Calakmul was built to honor the gods.

The Maya also believed in a sacred force called *k'uh*. Every person and object held *k'uh*. But rulers had the closest connection to the gods. Each city's ruler was known as *k'uhul ajaw*. This name meant "holy lord." People believed their ruler served as a link between them and

PEOPLE OF MAIZE

In one Maya **myth**, the gods needed three tries to create humans. First, they tried making people out of mud. But these people couldn't move or think. So, the gods destroyed them. They made new people from wood and grass. But those people would not honor the gods. The gods destroyed them, too. Then the gods made people from maize, or corn. These people became the first humans.

This stone carving shows Lady Ik' Skull, one of the few women to rule a Maya city.

the gods. The ruler performed rituals to keep the gods happy. In return, the people served the ruler.

When a ruler died, a family member took his or her place. Most Maya rulers were men. But a few women ruled Maya city-states. These queens controlled the city and fought in battle.

The Maya recorded their history on stone monuments called stelae. Their writing told the main events in each ruler's life. Maya writing used symbols called glyphs. Each picturelike symbol stood for a word or phrase.

Many Maya rulers were skilled warriors. A strong ruler could wage war on weaker city-states and force them to pay **tribute**. Captured people could also be sacrificed to the gods.

A *sacbe* leads to a ruined palace in the city of Labna.

But city-states did not always fight. Many traded food and goods. Traders often traveled along a *sacbe*. This was a raised road made of stone. The Maya built these roads throughout their kingdoms. Some roads ran between cities. Others connected temples, pyramids, or other important sites.

CHAPTER 3

DAILY LIFE

Maya society was divided into three groups. The groups were the nobles, the middle class, and the commoners. Only one-fourth of people were part of the nobility and the middle class. The rest were commoners who worked the land.

Nobles came from the most powerful families. They held the city's best jobs.

Maya priests created the Madrid Codex. It shows religious practices and daily life.

They served as priests, military leaders, and government officials.

Nobles lived in large homes. They wore fine clothing and beautiful jewelry. However, their wealth came at a price. Noble blood was sacred. They had to give blood sacrifices. They pricked their skin and let their blood flow onto strips of bark. They then burned the bark to send smoke up to the gods.

Some middle-class people lived in the cities. Others lived in villages outside. Each family's home was made of several stone buildings. These included a house, a kitchen, and a bathhouse. Middle-class people often worked as soldiers, traders,

Many Maya buildings were decorated with stone carvings.

or local officials. Others made and sold pottery, jewelry, carvings, and other objects.

Most commoners lived in villages. Their homes were built from clay and wood. They worked in the fields. They grew maize, squash, and beans. They also grew peppers and sweet potatoes.

 The Maya made vases from clay. They often painted scenes and patterns along the sides.

Women wove cloth and raised animals. When the growing season was over, many commoners traveled to the cities. They worked as builders or servants for noble families.

Maya life was filled with art. Artists carved huge statues and painted murals in temples and palaces. Nobles traded for smaller items, such as carved mirrors, for their homes. Even everyday objects like bowls and jugs had beautiful patterns.

CREATING CHOCOLATE

The Maya were the first people to make chocolate. Chocolate comes from cacao beans. People ground the beans and mixed them with water to make a drink. Unlike chocolate today, this drink was dark and bitter. The Maya did not have sugar. Instead, they added other flavors. They used chili, vanilla, or herbs. Cacao beans were valuable. People could trade the beans for other goods. Some rulers collected the beans as tribute.

CHAPTER 4

RISE AND FALL

Evidence of the Maya dates back to 1200 BCE. These early people lived in small groups and farmed the land. They became one of the first cultures to use **terrace** farming. This practice created more farmland in mountainous areas.

Over time, the Maya built villages and cities. Their earliest city was El Mirador.

A stela shows the history of a Maya city-state.

23

It was built more than 2,000 years ago. The Maya came to full power between 250 and 900 CE. During this time, huge cities rose in the jungle. They included El Tajín, Tikal, Copan, and Calakmul.

Palenque was another important Maya city. Its greatest ruler was K'inich Janaab Pakal. He became king in 615 CE. He was only 12 years old. His mother helped him rule the city for many years. When Pakal became king, Palenque was just a medium-sized city. But under his rule, it grew large and powerful. The people called him Pakal the Great.

Maya cities traded with one another. They also fought. In 695 CE, the cities

Parts of the palace and temples at Palenque still stand today.

of Tikal and Calakmul were locked in a bitter war. Tikal won. Its ruler, Jasaw Chan K'awiil, became a great king. Under his rule, the Maya built pyramids and other huge structures.

Around 850 CE, changes began taking place throughout the Maya kingdoms. In some places, ruling families began to die out. Other areas faced war or **drought**. As a result of these changes, the Maya began leaving their cities. They moved to the surrounding lands.

MAYA MATH

The Maya made many discoveries in math and science. They were some of the first people to understand the concept of zero. They also studied the movements of the sun, moon, and planets. Maya priests built observatories. They used these buildings to view objects in the night sky. The priests created many detailed charts. They could even predict **eclipses** of the sun and moon.

The Maya used this observatory at Chichen Itza to study the planet Venus.

By 950 CE, the great Maya cities were empty. Many cities became lost in the jungle. Plants grew over temples and pyramids. Meanwhile, the Maya people became farmers. Many never left their homelands. In fact, their **descendants** still live in these areas today.

CONTRIBUTIONS

MAYA CALENDARS

The Maya created a system of calendars to track the cycles of life. One was the Haab calendar. Farmers used this calendar to know when to plant crops. The calendar had 365 days. It followed the solar year, just like modern calendars do.

The Haab calendar had 18 months. Each month had 20 days. But that only adds up to 360 days. A calendar needs 365 days to match the sun's movement. So, the Maya added five days after the last month. These days were considered unlucky.

The Tzolk'in calendar was 260 days long. It followed nine cycles of the moon. A cycle is the time it takes for the moon to go from new moon to new moon again. The Maya used the Tzolk'in calendar to plan religious ceremonies.

Other calendars kept track of longer periods. One, known today as the Long Count, lasted

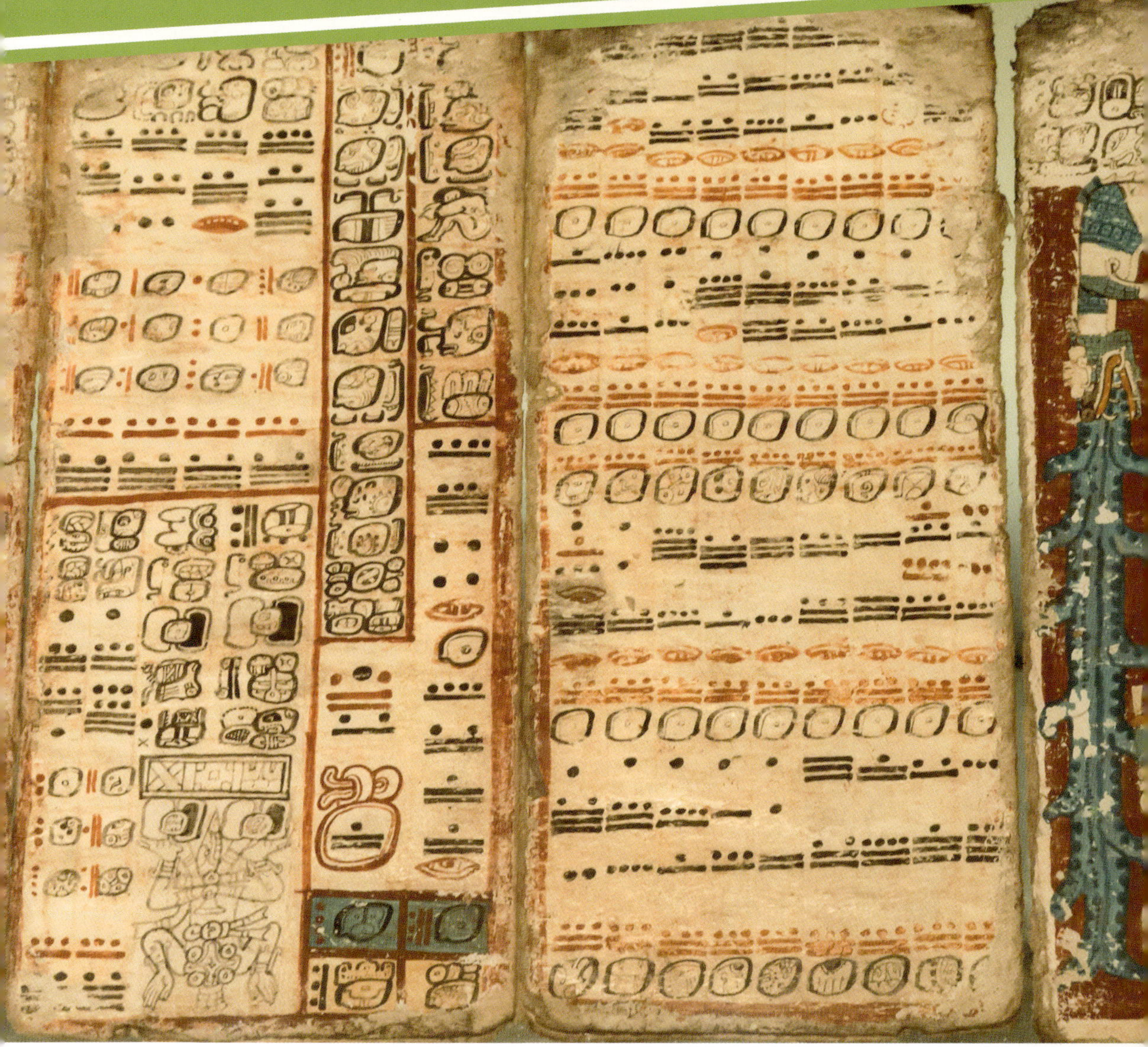

The Dresden Codex records the cycles of the Maya's 260-day calendar.

roughly 5,125 years. The Maya used this calendar to record important dates in history. These dates were often carved on stelae.

FOCUS ON
MAYA CIVILIZATION

Write your answers on a separate piece of paper.

1. Write a sentence summarizing the impact of one person described in Chapter 4.

2. Each Maya city had its own government. How would this system have helped the Maya people? How might it have been a problem?

3. What was the name of the ball game the Maya played?
    - **A.** *k'uh*
    - **B.** *pitz*
    - **C.** *sacbe*

4. Why might a drought have caused the Maya to leave their cities?
    - **A.** With less rain, they might have struggled to sail along rivers.
    - **B.** With less rain, they might have wanted shorter houses.
    - **C.** With less rain, they might have needed more land to grow crops.

Answer key on page 32.

GLOSSARY

civilization
A large group of people with a shared history, culture, and form of government.

descendants
People who come from a particular family, ancestor, or group of people.

drought
A period of dry weather.

eclipses
Times when light from the sun or moon is blocked from reaching Earth.

myth
A story about early history, especially one that involves supernatural beings or events.

sacrificed
Offered to the gods in exchange for protection or power.

terrace
A long, flat area along a mountainside created by building a wall.

tribute
Something valuable that one group is forced to give to a more powerful group.

TO LEARN MORE

BOOKS

Edwards, Sue Bradford. *Ancient Maya*. Minneapolis: Abdo Publishing, 2015.

Kule, Elaine A. *Exploring the Ancient Maya*. Mankato, MN: 12-Story Library, 2018.

Spilsbury, Louise. *The Mayans*. Chicago: Heinemann Raintree, 2017.

NOTE TO EDUCATORS

Visit **www.focusreaders.com** to find lesson plans, activities, links, and other resources related to this title.

INDEX

Ah Mun, 11
art, 21

calendars, 28–29
Chaac, 11
Chichen Itza, 5, 8
chocolate, 21

El Mirador, 23

gods, 6, 9, 11–14, 18

Itzamná, 11

Jasaw Chan K'awiil, 25

K'inich Janaab Pakal, 24
k'uh, 12

maize, 12, 19
math, 26

nobles, 17–18, 20–21

observatories, 26

Palenque, 8, 24
pitz, 5–7, 9
pyramids, 9, 15, 25, 27

sacbe, 15
sacrifice, 6, 14, 18
stelae, 14, 29

temples, 9, 15, 21, 27
Tikal, 8–9, 24–25
tribute, 14, 21

Answer Key: **1.** Answers will vary; **2.** Answers will vary; **3.** B; **4.** C